PAINLESS
CHILDBIRTH

An All-Natural Nutrition Plan

Patricia Antoine NHC

ISBN 978-1-959182-63-4 (paperback)
ISBN 978-1-959182-64-1 (hardcover)
ISBN 978-1-959182-71-9 (digital)

It is not the intent of the authors to prescribe or dispense medical advice. This book does not take the place of medical advice. Always consult a qualified physician or health practitioner. This book is for information only.

PSA Imprint
kauaiforyou@gmail.com

Printed in the United States of America

DEDICATION

To all women who are planning to become mothers and experience natural childbirth.

May this book inspire you to have natural childbirth and give your unborn child the best of everything to begin his/her new life on this earth.

Always remember that children are a special gift from God and giving them a healthy start in life is one of the best way parents can show love care and affection for this child.

ABOUT THE AUTHOR

I was born and raised on the island of Tobago, West Indies. I moved to the United States and shared six children with my spouse Dr. Carlisle Antoine

I studied Nutrition and do research in herbology and herbal formulation. I completed my doctors degree in Naturopathic Nutrition and Natural Health Consultant. I am also a home school educator and mom. I worked along with my husband for more than 25 years. I have done extensive research in Nutrition, Natural Medicine, natural childbirth and practice what I have learnt. Using these natural methods have been very effective not only with me but with friends whom we have help in their quest for health and Natural childbirth.

We have all experience painless childbirth and I wanted to share this with as many people as possible so they too can experience the joy of painless childbirth.

CONTENTS

INTRODUCTION

Children are a special gift from God. When couples decide to have children, one of the things they want most is to have a healthy child. The health of both mother and father is essential to having a healthy baby. It is important that the genes from both parents are well nourished with the right combination of diet, medicinal herbs, vitamins, and minerals. Not only is this a critical component to the health of the child, it can change your birth experience as well.

Painless Childbirth is another benefit of following the principles of health and taking the right combination of medicinal herbs, vitamins and minerals. It may sound too good to be true but one can experience a difference in childbirth as I did. A healthy pregnancy, a healthy baby, and a pleasant birthing process are absolutely achievable.

I have always contemplated the nature of childbirth and thought the process was just overwhelming. I decided to research the herbal formulas that play a significant role in the reproductive process. Armed with the formulas I discovered, I then combined them in such a strategic way that they complemented each other. The chemical constituents of these herbs not only nutrify the reproductive organs, but also allow for easy contraction and expansion.

There are essential factors one should take into consideration before pregnancy. At least six months to one year both parents should prepare themselves for this wonderful experience. Doing this dramatically reduces the risk for miscarriage, birth defects and other childhood dysfunctions.

Naturally painless (with minor discomfort at delivery) childbirth is something that can be accomplished by using the right herbal formulas, having a wholesome diet, regular exercise, lots of rest, drinking pure water, reading God's word and wholesome books and fortifying trust in God. I have personally used this program and have shared it with friends and we have all experienced painless childbirth.

Once you have followed the program outlined in this booklet, you will experience childbirth in a different way.

MY STORY

When I first learned about cleansing the immune system, I realized that it was a very important factor to being healthy and having a strong immune system. I love being healthy and strong. I mostly had a plant base diet and enjoyed eating lots of fresh fruits, greens and vegetables.

During my first pregnancy I experienced morning sickness and vomited for about 1 week. I knew about cleansing but did not do one before I got pregnant and so I could not do one at this time I did not know enough about natural child birth. I knew enough about nutrition and so I eat as healthy as I can and made sure I went for walks for my exercise. I did take a natural Multi-Vitamin and vitamin C but not much else. I felt pretty good and strife to maintain a positive attitude and spent time reading good books and the Bible. When I went into labor I experienced pain every time I had a contraction and as it was getting closer to deliver the pain increased and while in the hospital I was in much pain. I taught to myself there must be a better way than going through so much pain. Delivery was very painful and I tore and did not like the after effect of it.

After my first child, I decided to study midwifery and learn all I could about natural pre-natal care and to complement the nutrition I was studying.

I went on a complete body cleanse a year and half after my first child, made some changes to my diet and I truly felt stronger, healthier and more energetic. I then suspected I was pregnant because I missed my cycle. One thing I observed, when I became pregnant, is that I did not have any morning sickness. The prior cleansing and building of my immune system had prepared my body for the process of bearing this child.

With this new pregnancy I decided to apply what I have studied and learned about herbal formulas for pregnancy; the implementation of exercise, pure water, fresh fruits, vegetables, nuts, grains, legumes, sprouts, veggie meats and other unprocessed foods. Because of this, I had lots of energy and was able to do everything normal, as when I was not pregnant. I took care of my two year old son, cooking, cleaning and doing everything a mother would do. I did not feel any extreme tiredness or exhaustion at the end of the day. I realized that the combination of everything I was doing allowed my body to adjust to pregnancy, as a normal process of a woman's body.

Nine months into this second pregnancy, I was making dinner when I felt my first contractions. They felt like muscle contraction but without pain. I check the time and decided to finish my dinner and see how they progressed. About 7pm that evening I was still having contraction. After drinking my raspberry tea, the contraction became stronger and closer together but still without pain. The tightening of the muscles and pressure on the lower part of my abdomen were not accompanied by the pain of a typical pregnancy. After checking the time on the contractions I was feeling, I saw they were coming five minutes apart. I told my husband it was time to go to the hospital.

When I got to the hospital, The nurse asked me if I was sure I was in labor, due to my countenance; I did not look like I was in pain; but after she hooked up the monitor she realized that I truly was in labor. Once my water broke I felt only pressure and minimal pain. By the time I delivered my daughter, I was not exhausted and the following day I was released from the hospital.

This experience prompted me to share with others the joy of having children without the pain most experience. My next four children were born at home with a mid-wife for my third child and my husband for the last three. I did not have any morning sickness and always fortified my body with the right nutrients for a safe and pleasant experience.

During the delivery of my other four children at home I did hydrotherapy, to enable easier stretching of the tissues and prevent tearing. The range of my babies weight at birth were from 8.4 pounds to 12 pounds.

During hydrotherapy, when the head is seen at the vaginal opening, one must not push, but hold off and at that time dip a sterilized white wash cloth in warm water, squeeze out the excess water and place the cloth at the sides of the vaginal opening. This should be done at least three times or more if needed. Then one can push when the urge comes.

My experience with childbirth is one that I cherish because I know that God has truly given us the tools and knowledge to help us have a wonderful experience at childbirth.

Following this natural plan helps take the fear out of childbirth and gives one the confidence needed to have a pleasant experience and be fortified with wisdom and knowledge.

HOW TO HAVE PAINLESS CHILDBIRTH

One of the first things that **both parents** should do is to detoxify or cleanse their immune system. This must be done **before pregnancy.** If one is already pregnant, cleansing **cannot be done**. In this case it is best just to drink the teas, take the recommended vitamins and minerals, and follow the diet plan (page 18). This will make your pregnancy significantly easier and enjoyable.

The whole body cleanse will clean the entire chemistry and prepare the body for better absorption and transportation of nutrients. It is a special cleanse that can be purchased from e-mailing **kauaiforyou@ gmail.com,** for more information.

This cleanse is designed for working, non-working or busy people as well as mothers working at home. It does not cause diarrhea and work synergistically with the immune system. It will cleanse the whole immune system and will cause better nitrogen and oxygen transportation, more energy, and a healthier immune system.

For those unable to obtain this cleanse: You can check in your area for the best cleanse available and use a diet of fresh fruits and vegetables both steamed and in juice form for 1 week. (For further information and advice you can use the email above. Or you can consult with a Naturopathic Doctor.

After cleansing the system, it is then time for both parents to build their immune system and the mother to prepare her body for child bearing. A wholesome diet with lots of fresh fruits, vegetables, juices, raw salads, nuts grains, legumes, greens, ground foods (taro or dasheen, sweet potato, cassava, eddoes, etc.), veggie meats, organic non GMO tofu, and any kind of foods that are organic and not processed. (See Diet Guide pg. 18). A good multi-vitamin, vitamin C, B-complex should be taken daily by both parents for at least thirty to sixty day. If you live in an area where you cannot find all these foods and supplements try to eat as natural as possible and utilize all the fresh foods available in your area.

After rebuilding your system the body is now fortified for childbearing. When the wife conceives, the mother will begin to prepare herself for one of the most wonderful experience in her life. Continue your diet and add the herbs, vitamins and minerals. (see page 16 & 18)

This time is the most important of the unborn child's life. Special care needs to be taken at this time. We are what we eat, and therefore, if you eat a wholesome, high quality diet, it will fortify the health of both mother and child. The body will be able to produce healthy cells and form blood that will be rich and well oxygenated. Also special vitamins, mineral, herbs, and juices should be taken during this time. Red raspberry is very important to take during and after pregnancy (See recipe on how to make raspberry tea pg. 31). The following recommendation should be followed as closely as possible.

RECOMMENDED VITAMINS AND MINERALS

Natural Multi-Vitamin - One twice daily (Note: use either Douglas lab brand Energy/Sport or Nature's Plus brand or one that is comparable).

B-Complex (100mg) - One daily

B6 - 200 mg daily (if one is nauseated take 300 mgs daily until it goes away.)

Vitamin C - 1000 mg three times daily

Folic Acid - 400 mcg daily

Calcium Magnesium Chelate - 1200 mg daily or 1 glass of carrot juice three times weekly.

Red Raspberry Tea (see recipe on page 31) - 4 to 6 cups daily or 6 capsules daily.

Vitamin E (optional) - 200 IUs daily (depending on Blood Pressure. If Blood pressure is high you should not take Vitamin E)

Zinc - 30 mg daily

DIET

A high quality diet should be followed:. One rich in organic foods, vegetables, fruits, nuts, seeds, grains, legumes, ground food (taro or dasheen, potatoes, cassava, jicama, turnips etc.) greens, and any other freshly grown foods in your area. Pure water should always be taken in daily, approximately half your body weight in ounces.

When combining your meals always eat protein first then carbohydrates and salad, or eat the protein together with the carbohydrate and then salad.

If you are on gluten free diets try to use the fresh fruits and vegetables and non-gluten products on the market.

If you have any biological problems such as diabetes: Always ensure to consult with your physician and try to eat the best foods for your condition.

DIET PROGRAM GUIDE

Upon Rising: Glass of pure water. After water one can have lemon juice or glass of pure fruit juice.

A cup of herbal tea such as red raspberry, and your favorite herb tea.

A glass of freshly made fruit or vegetable juice. No canned juice should be used.

After your morning drink, take a walk. If you are not use to walking start slowly by walking for five to ten minutes and each day increase the time until you can walk for at least 30 minutes. Or if you like working in the garden, try working for at least 30 minutes.

Upon returning from walking or gardening, take a shower to wash perspiration away and now you are ready for breakfast.

If you are very hungry in the morning try having some fruit or smoothie before your walk.

Breakfast:

- Whole grain cereal with organic oat, soy, almond or rice milk.
- Whole grain toasted bread, fresh fruits (any fruit in season).
- Whole wheat, spinach or corn tortilla with raw vegetables salad (chopped or shredded carrots, cabbage, broccoli, cauliflower, cucumber, tomatoes, sprouts), beans, vegan cheese and veggie meat.

- Bowl of fresh fruits and berries. Nuts (walnuts, almond, sunflower seeds, cashews, Brazils nuts), raisins or dates.
- Veggie sandwich with lettuce, tomatoes, spinach, carrots, alfalfa sprouts, clover sprouts. Tapioca pudding.
- Whole grain, banana, yucca, or potato pancakes or waffles with raw unfiltered honey or pure maple syrup, fruits, handful of nuts, scrambled tofu, raw salad or Quinoa salad.
- Bowl of raw oatmeal soaked in milk (organic soy, almond, or rice), handful of raisins or 3 dates, and 3 prunes (fruit can be added to oatmeal).
- Handful of mixed nuts (unsalted), whole grain flakes, flax seeds or chia seeds with soy, almond or rice milk. Whole grain sandwich with sprouts, tomatoes, lettuce, veggie meat and vegan mayonnaise.

Lunch:

- Baked or boiled potatoes, steamed, mixed vegetables, raw salad, tofu, veggie meat or bulgur wheat, or taro or poi.
- Bowl of freshly prepared peas, or bean soup with vegetables, sweet potato, dumplings, and taro. Hay stack (pinto beans, black beans, organic chips, lettuce, spinach, tomatoes, olives, carrots, veggie meat or tofu, non-dairy cream cheese or sour cream.
- Brown rice with your favorite beans or peas, raw salad mix, steamed Brussel sprouts and veggie meat. Glass of freshly made vegetable or fruit juice.
- Glass of health drink (see recipes, pg. 36) with whole grain sandwich (sprouts, lettuce, tomato, avocado and veggie patty.
- Whole wheat, or rice Lasagna, with stir fry vegetables, raw sprouted salad sprinkled with sunflower seeds. Garlic ginger tofu with sunflower seeds.
- Quinoa and brown rice, with black beans, or any favorite beans, baked sweet potato, yams and beets. Raw vegetable salad. Glass of fruit smoothie.

- Raw vegetable salad with bean and seed sprouts, sprinkled with lightly toasted sunflower seeds and croutons. Baked potatoes with veggie meat. Breadfruit salad with vegetables (made just like potato salad). Steamed greens, corn, peas, broccoli, sugar snaps, cauliflower with veggie sausage.
- Potato salad with mixed vegetables and veggie meat. Raw green vegetable salad. Whole grain pasta with steamed vegetables and organic tofu.
- Fruit smoothie, green, drink, or vegetable juice.
- Chow Mein with steamed vegetables, egg-plant tofu and raw salad.
- Pizza with vegan cheese, vegetables and veggie meat, topped with fresh sliced tomatoes.
- Enchilada with raw vegetable salad, corn tortillas with your favorite filling. Tacos with lettuce, veggie crumble meat, tomatoes, olives, plant base sour cream. Tamales
- Indian curry with samosas and vegetable salad or a fruit bowl.

Dinner:

- Whole grain sandwich (lettuce, tomatoes, sprouts, cucumber, tofu or veggie patty, sprout and sprinkled with nutritional flakes.
- Glass of freshly made vegetable juice or fruit juice or smoothie.
- Fruit salad. Or Vegetable salad.
- Watermelon
- Bowl of grain cereal with soy, rice or almond milk. Glass of health drink (See page 36). Tapioca pudding.
- Cookie or cracker with vegan dip.
- Vegetable Salad, topped with your favorite nut or seeds.
- Fruit Salad, Tapioca pudding, or vegan cookie.
- Popcorn or whole grain snack.

DESSERTS: Vegan - Ice Cream, Cake, Cookies, Baklava, Date Nut roll, apple pie, raisin bread, pumpkin pie, Cinnamon roll with pecans, and any other dessert naturally made without processed sugars.

SEVEN DAY PLAN FROM FOODS LISTED:

One food out of each section can be chosen for each meal. However, if you are accumulating gas in your system you should eat small meals every two to three hours instead of large meals. All available fresh fruits and vegetables can be used daily.

Always look for the fresh live foods and fruits, along with legumes and grains in your area.

Diet should be 80% raw and 20% cooked. The more raw foods consumed the better. Remember that raw foods are live and loaded with nutrients to fortify the body and make healthy cells.

The list of foods for breakfast, lunch and dinner can be interchanged. Your heaviest meal should be at breakfast, lighter at lunch and lightest at dinner.

Desserts can be eaten after breakfast, lunch or dinner, remember to allow enough time for digestion before bed time.

Always remember it is good to take a short walk after each meal because it helps with digestion.

These foods are suggested for a wholesome diet, however, depending on your area and country you may not find all these foods so choose the best you can find in your country and as far as possible in its natural state without pesticides.

NOTES ON USE

THINGS TO AVOID:

1. All processed and refined foods such as white flour, white sugar and all products made from them. Excessive consumption has been known to cause hardening of the arteries and constipation.
2. All sodas and drinks made with processed sugars. These can cause much harm to the body and possible affect the pancreas.
3. All hydrogenated fats and excess of saturated fats. They are harmful to the immune system.
4. Overeating. Causes discomfort and stomach problems.
5. All dairy milk, cheese and products made with them. May affect the stomach, cholesterol level and weight. (if you have to use dairy use organic milk and meats)
6. Coffee, tea and any products made with caffeine. Affects the antioxidants and nerves in the system.
7. Smoking and second hand smoking. This constricts the arteries and has been known to cause cancer and problems for developing children.
8. Avoid STRESS AS MUCH AS POSSIBLE. Affects the whole immune system.
9. All unclean meats such as pork, shrimp, lobster, shell fish etc. (Read Leviticus 11 and Deuteronomy 14). These may cause different biological problems.
10. Most canned fruits and vegetables. They are denatured.

11. Table salt and products made with them. Salt tend to settle in the brain, interfere with memory and can cause high blood pressure.
12. Overexertion and lack of sleep. Interferes with the rebuilding of healthy cells.
13. Drugs of all forms. Damages the immune system.
14. Microwave foods. Changes the monocular structure of the foods making it foreign to the body.

DO NOT USE ANY ALUMINUM, TEFLON OR COPPER COOKING UTENSILS. These utensils are not good to cook with because when damaged or overheated can cause chemical to enter food. Only use clay, glass, iron or stainless steel.

THINGS TO USE:

- Use only cold pressed vegetable oils such as safflower oil, flax seed oil and olive oil. For salt substitute use vege-sal seasoning salt or any other natural salt substitute that is comparable.
- Use raw honey, stevia, maple syrup, sucanat or molasses for sweetener. If you have diabetes the best sweetener is stevia.
- Try to find the most natural veggie meats.
- Exercise is very important and should be done at least three to five days per week. The best form of exercise is walking. When starting out walk slowly and take deep breaths. Every day, increase your speed and length of time you walk. Do not overexert or tired yourself.
- Try to rest daily.
- Only use soy, oat, rice, or almond milk and soy, rice or almond cheeses without casein. The reason for not using dairy is because dairy milk is mucous forming and will affect the unborn child. He/she will be more susceptible to colds and flus and infection.
- Fresh fruit and fruit juices are high in antioxidant and can be used in combination with ginger tea.

- Raw vegetables and vegetable juice are nourishing for daily use. Always try to have raw foods with each meal.
- Always remember deep breathing exercises are very important and doing this daily, will help you to have more oxygen in the cells and tissues of the body. This will also help both you and the unborn child.
- On the onset of contraction drink your Red Raspberry tea as this will help you to have a smooth delivery. If it is true labor, the tea will aid the body as well.

NOTE: If you live in a country where almond, rice, or soy milk are not available, use goat's milk rather than cow's milk. Goat's milk is not mucous forming. You can also use Goat cheese. If you have to eat meat, choose grass fed organic meats and poultry.

HERBS

Herbs are very beneficial to the mother and child. It aids the body in replenishing vital nutrients and also strengthens the body for delivery.

Red raspberry, alfalfa, kelp and dandelion are some that have been used with great success in pregnancy.

Alfalfa, kelp and dandelion, in combination, are an excellent source of iron to take. One should take four capsules daily. Another iron is Floradix iron plus, this comes in liquid form and is very beneficial to the mother.

During the last six weeks of pregnancy herbs like alfalfa, oat straw, blessed thistle, black cohosh, squaw vine, and acacia can be taken because of their high calcium content and the ability to aid the body at this time. Calcium is very important for the formation of strong bones.

****

Caution: <u>Do not use</u> the following herbs during pregnancy: Aloe Vera, Don Quai, wild yam, parsley, Pennyroyal, Rue, hash laxatives, Senna, cascara sagrada, bitter melon and any other herbs which contain steroids. They can harm the mother and the child.

GOOD SOURCES OF PROTEIN, NATURAL FATS, COMPLEX CARBOHYDRATE, VITAMINS, AND MINERALS.

LEGUMES	VEGETABLES	NUTS & SEEDS	GRAINS
Beans	Asparagus	Almonds	Barley
Garbanzos	Broccoli	Cashew	Buckwheat
Lentils	Brussels sprouts	Sesame seeds	Corn
Kidney bean	Collards, Kale	Sunflower seed	Millet
Peas	Carrots	Walnuts	Oats
Soybeans	Tomatoes	Pecans	Brown rice
Pintos	Spinach	Pumpkin seed	Amaranth
String beans	Bok choy	Brazil nut	Spelt
Mung beans	Chard	Breadnut	Quinoa
Spanish beans	Pumpkins	Filbert	Teff
Green beans	Cabbage	Chestnut	Kamut

Nutritious Fruits:

Apples, bananas, mangoes, black berry, blue berry, cantaloupe, cherry, plums, figs, peaches, mangosteen, papaya, atemoya, custard apple, nectarine, guava, grapefruit, oranges, grapes, pomegranate, tangerine, pineapple, strawberry, pears, and any other fruit that is found in your region.

Nutritious Vegetables:

Asparagus, beets, bell peppers, broccoli, Brussels sprouts, cabbage, carrots, cauliflower, celery, cucumbers, eggplant, fennel, garlic, leeks, mushrooms, mustard greens, olives, onions, potatoes, lettuce, squash, Swiss chard, turnips, tomatoes, kale, pak-choi, collard greens and any fresh vegetables found in your area.

BREASTFEEDING

Breastfeeding is one of the most rewarding health benefit a mother can give to her child. Due to breastfeeding, my children hardly ever got sick in their young childhood years and very rarely caught a cold or suffered from allergies.

Early breast milk enables the child to resist many kinds of illnesses. It gives the child colostrum which is loaded with nutrients and antibodies, to protect the child and keep the body healthy. Breast milk is easier to digest, than cow's milk and baby formula; it allows the baby to have a stronger immune system.

Mother's milk composition varies over the course of lactation. In the first few days colostrum is produced and it has a yellowish color because it cantains high levels of beta carotene (approximately 10 times more than mature milk)

Colostrum also contains vitamin E, zinc, calories B 12, protein fats and carbohydrates. It has thyroxine which increases over the first week helping the baby's intestine and metabolism to develop. Leptin is high in the first 180 days to control weight and appetite and influences healthy microbial flora.

Each time one breast feeds, one release relaxing and bonding hormones oxytocin which has a calming effect on the baby and benefits both baby and mother long after weaning to help prevent heart diseases.

Oligosaccharide feeds the baby's intestines and keep a healthy digestive bacteria flora. This constantly changes from day to day through the mother's milk to help the baby develop a healthy digestive system.

Some research has been shown that breastfeeding, can help reduce the risk of SIDs (sudden infant death syndrome), Type I diabetes and even childhood leukemia. (http://www.llli.org/faq/prevention.html)

These and other diseases can be prevented if the mother follows the plan in this book and breastfeed the baby until at least 12 to 18 months. This helps in the development of the child and allows the child to grow strong and healthy while bonding with the mother.

I want to encourage every mother to breastfeed because this is one way you can give your child the much needed nourishment to resist diseases and other ailments and spend these precious moment forming a bond that will last a lifetime.

To enrich and produce more milk the following herbs has been proven to be safe and effective.

Red raspberry, alfalfa, fennel, Blessed Thistle and chlorophyll. (See section on recipes pg. 31)

When one is ready to stop breastfeeding using parsley, kelp or sage tea will help to dry up the milk.

SUMMARY

Ask God for wisdom, knowledge and understanding, and spend time reading wholesome books that will edify your mind and give you pleasant thoughts and help your baby to be happy. Both husband and wife should cleanse and build their immune system before having a child. Always drink at least 6 – 8 cups of pure water daily.

Develop an exercise program that will fit your needs. Walking is one of the best ways to exercise. Walk for at least thirty minutes. Deep breathing exercises are very helpful.

One should get at least 10 to 20 minutes of sunshine daily this help in your Vitamin D absorption.

Eat a well-balanced, healthy diet with at least 80% raw and 20 % cooked foods.

Always take your vitamins, minerals, herbs and raspberry tea every day during your pregnancy.

Eat lots of fresh fruits, vegetables and greens.

Have at least 8 hours sleep.

Keep a loving, cheerful, calm spirit.

Always make sure that the food you choose to eat is unprocessed and as much as possible, used in its natural form. I would recommend not using any GMO foods.

A positive attitude and happy laughter is healthy medicine for the soul, and when you are carrying this precious bundle of joy, maintaining this kind of attitude is very helpful to the child.

As you venture on this journey always remember that children are a blessing from God. This diet is a guide and you can choose to add other healthy unprocessed foods that may not have been mentioned.

Breastfeeding your baby is also very beneficial for you and your child.

In order to experience this new discovery, the guidelines given in this book can aid you in having a wonderful experience during childbirth.

RED RASPBERRY

Red Raspberry tea is known as nature's best herb for mothers. This herb is to be taken throughout the pregnancy and after especially when breastfeeding. It aids the body in preventing miscarriages and fortifies the body with nutrients and trace minerals needed during and after childbirth. It also helps in the production of mother's milk.

HOW TO PREPARE RED RASPBERRY TEA:

Red Raspberry leaf: In a glass or stainless steel pot put two ounce of raspberry leaf and two and a half pints of water. Bring to a boil, turn off burner and let steep for 30 minutes. Strain and drink one tea cup two times daily in your first trimester, three cups in the second trimester and the final three months drink at least four to six cups daily. Do not use tea bags as they do not have the potency as the loose herbs.

If you cannot drink tea and can find red raspberry capsules, take four every day in the first three months, take six capsules the second three months and in the last three months take 9 capsules daily. This as I mentioned before is one of the best herb a mother can use and it is crucial in helping both mother and child during pregnancy

For increasing breast milk production do the following:

1 Tablespoon red raspberry
1 Tablespoon fennel
1 Tablespoon blessed thistle
2 pints of boiling water.

Put herbs into boiling water, turn off burner, cover and let steep for 30 minutes, strain and sweeten with honey, stevia or cane juice. Store in the Refrigerator. One tea cup daily is recommended or two if needed. This tea is recommended two to three months after the baby is born.

Milk production will increase, and this tea should only be used if you are not producing enough milk for the baby.

This tea enriches mother's milk and will sustain and help the baby to sleep through the night at an earlier age.

Do not drink more that two cups in one day. Once the milk starts coming in only drink as needed (possible every other day or week depending on milk production)

For question or advice you can email me at the following email: kauaiforyou@gmail.com.

RECIPES

JUICES

Vegetables juices:

- 2 carrots, 3 kale leaves, 1 apple, ¼ piece beet, ½ cucumber, 1 small piece of cabbage, 1 apple.
- 2 carrots, ½ cucumber, ¼ beet, ½ apple.
- 2 cups organic spinach, ½ cup pineapple, 3 cups apple juice
- 3 carrots, ¼ beet with greens, 1 stalk celery, hand full of spinach
- ¼ cabbage, 2 carrots, ½ cucumber, 3 leaves kale (avocado can be added for richness)

Juice any <u>one</u> of these in a juicer or Vita Mix and drink for your health and that of the baby. Other vegetable juices can be used,.

<u>Do not use parsley</u> in your drinks because it can prevent milk from forming. These juices should be taken at least once a day. If juicing in a Vita Mix add either water or apple juice for liquid.

Fruit Juices:

- 1 inch thick round pineapple, 7 strawberries, ½ banana, 1 apple
- 1 orange, ½ lime, ½ kiwi (peeled), 1 cup apple juice
- ½ cup blueberries, 1 orange, ½ banana, ¾ cups water
- 8 strawberries, ½ banana, 7 blue berries, ¼ piece pineapple
- 1 peeled orange, ½ banana, ¼ piece pineapple,

- 1 pack acai berry, 1/3 cup blue berry, 7 strawberry, ½ banana, (1 cup of milk or apple juice can be added for blending)
- 1 cup mangoes, ¼ cup pineapple, 7 strawberries, 12 blue berries, ½ banana, 1 cup apple juice.

Frozen fruits can be used to make these fruit juices also. Apple juice must be added before blending. For a richer drink add ½ scoop of Spirutein Protein powder (your favorite flavor) or you can use your favorite protein powder.

You can use stevia, honey or cane juice to sweeten smoothies if needed.

Any available fresh or frozen fruits can be used to make fruit juices or smoothies.

Both vegetables and fruits drinks provide lots of live organic nutrients and nourish not only the mother but the baby as well. Always try to use organic fruits and vegetables because they are grown without pesticides.

NOTE: If you are allergic to certain greens or fruits do not use them.

TROPICAL BLEND SMOOTHIE

4 cups tropical fruits (pineapple, banana, mango, strawberry etc)
1/2 frozen banana
2 scoops vanilla sherbet
5 cups apple juice
2 ounces dehydrated cane juice (optional)
1 scoop Spirutein Protein powder

Blend all ingredients and serve. Different fruits can be substituted and made into smoothies.

****

Each of these fruits is high in vitamins and minerals and also gives energy to the body.

HEALTH DRINK

3 cups soy, almond, or rice milk
1 scoop Spirutein Protein Powder
1 tsp. vanilla or almond essence
2 blocks Irish Moss (optional)
10 pieces walnuts (optional)
12 almonds (optional)
¼ teaspoon vege-sal (optional)

HONEY TO TASTE

Any favorite fruit can be added. (except citrus). Frozen fruits can be used.

Also two tablespoons of oats can be added to make it into a breakfast drink.

BLEND AND SERVE CHILL WITH CRUSH ICE. (Optional)

This drink is very nourishing, high in fiber, vitamins and minerals.

CHICKEN-LIKE SEASONING

1 1/3 cups nutritional yeast flakes
3 Tbsp. onion powder
2 1/2 tsp. garlic powder
2 Tbsp. Vege-Sal seasoning
2 tsp. celery seeds
2 Tbsp. Italian seasoning
1 Tbsp. parsley flakes

Blend all ingredients until smooth. Store in a glass container: Use to flavor in soup, gravy, patties etc. Also use to make chicken broth and used on pasta.

****

Nutritional flakes are rich in vitamins, (especially B-vitamins, minerals), and are a complete protein.

Celery seeds are rich in calcium, magnesium, potassium, zinc and vitamin C.

PARMESAN CHEESE

2 cups almonds (lightly toasted and grounded)
1 cup sesame seeds (crushed)
1 cup nutritional yeast flakes (powdered)
1 tsp. Vege-Sal seasoning

Combine all ingredients together and store in a glass jar in the refrigerator.

****

These nutrients combined are rich in calcium, vitamins, and minerals and are a complete protein.

It is excellent to put on top of pizzas, pastas and sandwiches.

For a cheese spread do the following:

In a Vita Mix, put 1 carrot, ¼ cup cashews, and crush. Now add ½ cup of milk or creamer, (non-dairy), ¼ cup parmesan cheese. Blend, and while blending slowly add 1/3 cup vegetable oil.

Stop adding oil when desire texture is reached. Refrigerate and use within a week.

WHOLE WHEAT CAROB CAKE

2 Tbsp olive oil (optional)
6 ounces Earth Balance butter
8 ounces sucanat (dehydrated cane juice)
1 large apple (crushed)
1 Tbsp. vanilla extract (optional)
1 tsp almond extract
1 tsp cinnamon (optional)
3/4 cup whole wheat pastry flour
1 cup unbleached white flour
¼ cup carob powder
1 Tbsp baking powder (non-almininum) pinch of grated lemon rind

Topping

1/2 cup almonds (crushed)
1 ounces butter
2 Tbsp. sucanat

Mix together and set aside.

In a large mixing bowl, beat and oil butter until light and fluffy. Add sugar and beat well. Add crushed apple and mix. Now add extract, lemon rind and mix. Add dry ingredients mix well. Lightly spray a 9 in cake pan and pour mixture. Add toping.

Pre-heat oven to 350 degrees and bake for 30 minutes. Turn off oven and leave in heat for 5 minutes, then remove. Cool and serve.

VEGETABLE SALAD

1/2 small green cabbage (finely chopped)
1/2 small purple cabbage (finely chopped)
2 large carrots (grated or shredded)
1 stalk broccoli (diced)
1/2 small Cauliflower (chopped)
1 cup baby spinach
1/2 cup alfalfa sprouts
1/2 cup clover sprouts
3 large tomatoes (cubed)
7 leaves lettuce (chopped)
1/2 can slice olives (optional)
1/2 cup sunflower seed (lightly toasted or raw)
2 ounces olive oil or safflower oil
1/4 piece onion (grated)
Salt to taste with Vegesal seasoning

In a large bowl combine all ingredients, add olive oil or safflower oil with Vegesal seasoning to taste. Mix well, sprinkle sunflower seed on top and serve. This is a very delicious salad that can be eaten with a meal or by itself.

For a nice touch, croutons, cubed tofu, peas or beans can be added for a complete meal.

This is very high in fiber, vitamins and minerals

QUINOA SALAD

1 cup quinoa (cooked)
½ cup cilantro or shadow benne
4 cups tomatoes (cubed)
3 cup cucumber (cubed)
1 cup carrots (shredded or small cubed)
1/2 cup red or yellow sweet onion
1 jalapeno pepper or flavor pepper (seeded and chopped)
2 clove crushed garlic
2 Tbsp. Olive oil
1/8 tsp. cayenne (optional)
1/2 tsp. Vege-Sal seasoning
1 ½ ounces lemon juice (less can be used if desired)
1/2 cup lightly toasted sunflower seeds and/ or sesame seeds

HOW TO COOK QUINOA:

In a small pot put 1 cup of raw quinoa, 1 tablespoon onion powder, 1 teaspoon garlic powder, 2 tablespoon chicken style seasoning (see recipe on pg. 37), 1/2 teaspoon brags liquid amino, and 2 cups of water. Bring to a boil and reduce heat to medium low for 15 minutes uncovered. Then cover and let simmer for 10 to 15 minutes or until all water is absorbed. Remove from heat and let it steam. When cool, refrigerator overnight. Now you are ready to make your salad. Put cold quinoa in a medium size bowl and add all other ingredients except the sunflower seeds. Mix well, taste for salt, and if needed, add salt to taste. Sprinkle sunflower seeds or lightly toasted walnuts or pecans or sesame seeds on top and serve.

OAT MEAL COOKIES

6 ounces earth balance butter
2 tablespoons olive oil (optional)
8 ounces sucanat or dehydrated cane juice
1/2 cup soy milk
1 teaspoon mixed essence or vanilla or almond essence
1 cup unbleached white flour
1 cup whole wheat pastry flour
2 cups oats
2 teaspoons baking powder
1 teaspoon cinnamon
1/8 teaspoon nut meg

Pre-heat oven at 350 degrees.

In a large mixing bowl beat butter, sugar and oil until light. Add sugar, and mix. Now add milk and essence and mix well. Add flours, oats, baking powder, cinnamon, nutmeg and mix well.

Line a baking sheet with parchment paper.

Scoop cookie into the size you wish unto parchment paper and bake for 15 minutes. Turn oven off and leave in heat for 5 minutes. Remove from heat cool and serve.

SPINACH GREEN DRINK

2 cups organic baby spinach
1/2 cup pineapple cubes
3 cups apple juice
2 cups ice (optional)
Blend all ingredients and serve.

****

Spinach is rich in antioxidants, vitamin C, and chlorophyll. Apples are high in antioxidant and fiber. Pineapple is an excellent source of manganese, and contains the digestive enzyme bromelain.

BANANA NUT BREAD

2 cups frozen bananas
2/3 cup vegetable oil
1 apple peeled
1 cup sucanat (honey can be substituted or used half /half)
1 tsp vanilla or almond essence
1 cup whole wheat flour
1 cup unbleached flour
1 Tbsp baking powder (non aluminum)
1/2 chopped walnuts (Optional)
1/8 teaspoon vege-sal (optional)

Preheat oven at 350 degrees.

Blend bananas, oil, sugar and apple together until smooth. Pour in a large mixing bowl. Mix all dry ingredients together and slowly add to liquid mixture. Mix well. Now add nuts and mix.

Pour into a lightly sprayed 9 in baking dish and bake for 30 minutes. Turn off over and let sit in heat for 5 minutes. Remove from oven, cool and serve.

Bananas are a healthy source of fiber, potassium, vitamin B6, vitamin C, and various antioxidants and phytonutrients. Apples are also high in fiber and other vitamins. These are all heart healthy and help with energy.

Painless Childbirth, An All Natural Nutritional Plan shares the childbirth process and more through researched, into the importance of medicinal herbs during and after childbirth the author was able to experience firsthand the benefits of the techniques practiced in this book.

The diet, exercise, herbal formulas, vitamins and minerals detailed in this book will tremendously enhance your knowledge of what it is to experience a difference in childbirth.

As you read this book, may you realize that children are a special gift from God and each child should have the best of beginnings in their lives with love, tenderness, affection and care.

Please check out the video below:

https://www.youtube.com/watch?v=TLpbfOJ4bJU

Video shows how diet can affect the brain. This is from conception to adulthood.

www.ingramcontent.com/pod-product-compliance
Lightning Source LLC
Chambersburg PA
CBHW031259120626
46545CB00007B/2889